AF212003

JAKE BRETON

Ebooks for Income

The Ultimate Guide to Making Money from eBooks,
Discover How You Can Create Winning eBooks
That Generate Big Bucks

Descrierea CIP a Bibliotecii Naționale a României
JAKE BRETON
    Ebooks for Income. The Ultimate Guide to Making Money from eBooks, Discover How You Can Create Winning eBooks That Generate Big Bucks / Jake Breton. – Bucharest: Editura My Ebook, 2020
    ISBN

JAKE BRETON

eBooks for Income

**The Ultimate Guide to Making Money
from eBooks, Discover How You Can Create
Winning eBooks That Generate Big Bucks**

My Ebook Publishing House
Bucharest, 2020

TABLE OF CONTENTS

INTRODUCTION

If you want to make money online, then selling an ebook has to be one of the very best strategies there is. When you sell an ebook, you are selling your own product which right away helps you to maximize profits. You're not an affiliate or an advertiser; you're now right at the *top* of the pyramid as far as selling goes and you don't have to share your profits with anyone.

At the same time, when you sell an ebook, you keep people more attached to your brand. When you advertise, you are essentially being paid to send your visitors *away* from your pages. When you sell a product of your own conversely, the visitors are engaging with your brand much *more* and seeing even more evidence of your authority. If you sell an ebook and it's *good*, then you'll find it's even easier to sell more ebooks and other products in the future!

And as though that wasn't enough, ebooks also have the significant benefit of being completely free to produce and having no overheads or 'COGS' (Cost of Goods Sold). That means that all the revenue you generate from your ebooks will be 100% profit and it means that you won't lose any money if the book turns out not to sell! This is a completely risk-free business model with the lowest barrier to entry around. And as an added bonus, creating an ebook is something that anyone can do without needing any specialist skills or tools. If you know how to write and you have a basic word processor on your computer, then this is something you can build!

The Challenges and Why Now is the Perfect Time

Of course no business model is perfect however and there are obviously always going to be challenges that you'll face when creating any product and trying to sell it.

The biggest challenge when it comes to creating and selling ebooks, is demonstrating that your book will provide value and making sure that it's appealing to the widest possible audience.

Specifically, the problem with ebooks is that they don't appeal to everyone and that it can be hard to separate yourself from a lot of low quality products. Unfortunately, the fact that ebooks are so easy to create and so profitable, means that many people have taken advantage of the situation by selling spammy ebooks that don't really offer much value.

You've likely discovered this yourself if you've come across the thousands of adverts selling ebooks on getting abs or making money. Often when you download those ebooks, you'll find they contain barely any useful information and aren't particularly well written.

And even if this wasn't the case, it's still always a challenge trying to convince people who aren't tech savvy to download ebooks. For instance, it's probably quite unlikely that you'll be able to convince your Grandma to read books on her computer! And the same probably goes for your Dad, his work colleagues, a lot of your friends... This is a limited market. Or at least it is on the face of it!

With that said, now is actually the very best time to create and sell an ebook. Never have ebooks been as widely accepted or enjoyed by as wide a range of people. Partly the reason for this is down to the generally increased acceptance of ecommerce. Partly it's due to the increase in digital devices that are more portable and more suitable for reading ebooks. And partly it's because of the Kindle.

Did you know that Amazon has sold *more* digital books than hard copy books since 2010 thanks to the Kindle? And these appeal to a huge audience that includes office workers on their commutes, students and stay-at-home Mums!

There are over 4.3 million ebooks available in the US right now through Amazon and this number is increasing all the time. Then you have the countless ebooks sold through platforms like JVZoo and Clickbank... it's a good time to be an ebook author!

The key is simply to create an ebook that has as broad an appeal as possible and then to ensure that you can reach the broadest audience with the right marketing and advertising strategies. We'll look at how to do all those things right here!

By the end of this ebook, you will learn:

- How to create an ebook (either yourself, or by outsourcing)
- How to design a cover and pick a title
- How to price your book
- How to format and edit your book
- Where to market your book for maximum sales
- How to sell physical copies of your book!
- How to increase your sales and reach the largest possible audience
- How to sell ebooks from your website
- And much more!

Chapter 1

Choosing a Niche and Title That Will Sell

So now you know why ebooks are such a great way to make money and you know the state of the industry as it exists right now.

Let's not beat around the bush any further – let's dive straight into making your ebook so that you can start profiting!

And the best place to begin when it comes to creating a book is to come up with a title and a niche. In other words: what is your book going to be about? What will you call it? Who will it appeal to? And how will you market it?

This is perhaps the single most important decision when it comes to your book as it will actually impact on all the other aspects of your business. The niche of your book for instance will not only affect what you're writing about and what you need to know; it will dictate your target audience and in turn, where you are going to market it. It will dictate the marketing strategies you can use to sell it and it will even determine how much you can sell it for – some topics simply allow you to charge more than others because they offer bigger changes to the lifestyle and more impressive benefits.

Meanwhile, your title is what you will use to convey the niche, as well as to convey the 'value proposition' of your book (i.e. what you are claiming your book can do for people). Read on and we'll look at how to go about selecting the perfect niche for your book and then turning that into an ideal title.

Choosing Your Niche

When it comes to choosing your niche, there are a huge number of different factors to consider and a vast number of different ways you need to think about it.

The first and most obvious consideration in many cases is going to be what kind of business you are *already* running. In other words, if you already have a website or a blog, then you will most likely want to create a book that is based on the same subject matter so that you can sell to your same audience.

So if you have a blog that's all about fitness, making a fitness ebook is the logical decision. While you *could* try to sell an ebook on another topic, this would only make a lot more work for yourself unnecessarily; especially if you have already built a captive audience and developed a lot of trust with them!

If you don't have a blog or a website already though, then you need to think about the type of subject matter that you might be interested in. You're going to have to write at least 10,000 words to create your ebook (unless you outsource it) and even on top of that, you will need to create a lot of additional marketing material in order to promote the book. If this is a topic you know about, then you should find it's easy to bring something new to the table, to create marketing materials that demonstrate your expertise and to find the right ways to market yourself.

Conversely, if you pick a topic in which you have no experience, then you'll have a hard time contributing anything to the field and in all likelihood, you'll struggle to make any sales.

In fact, this is one of the biggest and most important considerations of all when choosing your niche. There are just *too many* people out there writing ebooks on topics that they think they can sell easily and with no experience on the matter.

The result?

The book essentially repeats itself for 10,000 words, the marketing materials make it obvious that there's nothing useful or interesting contained within the content and no one buys it. Likewise, the sellers often know themselves that they aren't providing much useful content and thus feel shy to promote it and even when they do make sales, they'll find lots of people demand a refund.

This is even more problematic if you try and sell a book on Kindle, as here people can read a free preview before they commit themselves to buying the product. As a result, they will see right away that you aren't offering anything new and they'll leave.

At this point you might be thinking: 'I'll just outsource the content'. Even here though, you're going to run into challenges. Because while you might hire the best writer in the world, chances are that they aren't an expert in the subject matter that you've chosen – unless they specifically state that they are.

You can't find a random writing agency and ask them to write you 'the definitive book on programming in C++'. Even if they know C++ or are able to learn it, it's hardly going to contend with all the books written by genuine experts.

So in short, you rally *should* be an expert on the niche you choose. And if you're not an expert, then at least pick a niche that you understand very well.

You should also decide whether you're going to be creating a definitive guide, or a book that offers a completely new perspective. The latter is harder to think up but much easier to create.

Look at it this way: if you're going to create a fitness ebook, then you need to compete with the thousands and thousands of fitness ebooks already on the market. How do you do that?

One option is to be 100% definitive. That means that you're going to aim to do a better job than all the other ebooks on the same subject and that you're going to write the official text that people will turn to when they want to know about that topic.

You can pick a subcategory of your main subject ('The Mediterranean Diet', 'Functional Strength Training', 'Fitness Trackers', 'Yoga') but ultimately your aim is still to offer something that's better than anything anyone else is putting out.

The alternative though is just to offer something completely new and different. That might mean that you invest your *own* fitness training program or your own breakthrough diet. It might mean that you tackle the subject of training in a new and unique way. Or it might mean that you target an audience who isn't usually catered for.

Really this boils down to your motivation for writing the book. If your motivation is to pick a topic you think will sell, you might be surprised to find it's actually quite difficult to convince people to buy from you. But if your motivation is to write something because you have an exciting new idea and you really want to contribute to the niche you're writing for, then you'll find you have a much bigger audience!

What are the Best Niches?

So factors outside of your control might define your niche. But that said, there are also a large number of specific topics that will be easier to sell and easier to make money from.

The most popular niches for ebooks written by marketers by far are:

- Fitness
- Dating
- Making money online

And the reason for this is that these topics all appeal to universal aims. All of us want money, all of us want to be healthy and all of us wish we could make money without going to work (we want financial independence).

Another way to say this, is that ebooks have a particularly appealing 'value proposition'. A value proposition is essentially what you promise your book can do for people and it's about how your book will change their lives.

People don't buy fitness books just because they want to be healthier. They buy them because they want to be confident in the way they look, because they want to feel attractive and because they want to wake up full of energy in the mornings. This is the emotion behind your product and it's what will help you to sell your books.

If your book is about knitting though, then your value proposition is a lot less emotive and life changing. People learn to knit as a way to busy themselves in the evening and as a fun pastime – they don't learn it to change their lives, their health or their relationships.

And for these reasons, you can't charge as much for a book on knitting as you can for a book on fitness.

But at the same time, books on fitness will face a *lot* more competition than books on knitting – because just about every internet marketer out there has a title on this subject.

Getting your book to stand out and get noticed is a big challenge then, which is why you need to use the advice given earlier to make your book more unique and to sidestep some of that competition. As mentioned before, you can do this by making your book on a specific subcategory of fitness or aiming it at a specific audience. Examples might be:

- Fitness for the over 50s
- Fitness for martial arts
- CrossFit
- Yoga
- Bikram Yoga
- The Mediterranean Diet
- Fitness for diabetics
- Etc.

Notice how the 'fitness for martial arts' topic actually combined two different subjects.

Even then though, you will struggle to find a specific route to market to promote your ebook and you will struggle to make it stand apart from other books in that niche. This is why many writers will still choose to tackle subjects that are less conventional and that don't have the same large emotional appeal.

I you write about knitting for instance, then you will find there is much less competition and that it's much easier to sell your book to a very specific group of people who will most likely gather in specific places (such as knitting forums). You just won't be able to charge as much and you'll likely have a smaller market before you reach saturation.

The ideal scenario then would be to find some kind of compromise. Choosing the 'niche within a niche' is one option but another would be to choose a niche such as a particular industry or career – or a skill that can be monetized.

For example, take the example of a book aimed at a specific type of industry: stage lighting, running a café, building apps, or making money as a personal trainer.

When you have a book like this you have a *very* specific niche and a very specific target audience. This gives you some easy options to market your book. At the same time, there are specific places where this audience will congregate where you can market yourself and sell your books. And on top of all this, an ebook on a career is something that *can* be used to help someone make money and that can therefore potentially change their lives.

People will be willing to pay a lot of money for an ebook on running their own restaurant if that is their dream – apart from anything else, they should make back the investment!

How To Choose An eBook Title

With all that in mind, the last thing to do is to come up with your title. And what's key here is that you choose a title that will reflect the content in the book and that will get people excited for it. This means that you need to express the 'value proposition' we already discussed, you need to highlight what sets your book apart and you need to make sure that you mention everything that is going to be covered.

So don't just call your book:

A Guide to Functional Fitness

As that really doesn't tell people about the book. Instead call it:

Functional Power: How to Use Functional Fitness to Develop Real, Useful Crushing Power. Conquer Sports and Transform Your Body!

This now hits home precisely what your book is about and it forces the reader to imagine how the book could potentially change their lives.

Similarly, you shouldn't call your book:

My Sushi Restaurant

Instead, call it:

My Sushi Restaurant: Your Business Model in 5 Simple Steps – Run Your Own Restaurant, Live Your Dreams and Cook Amazing Sushi!

Having a title and a subtitle like this means you can say everything you need to say, while still having a catchy few words for marketing purposes.

Chapter 2

Writing or Outsourcing Your Book Content

We devoted an awful lot of time to the niche and the title but hopefully you recognize just why this is so important. And if you gave this the proper thought that it deserves, then hopefully it should help you to populate your book with content and to understand precisely what will make the book a success.

In short, you need to focus on delivering that value proposition – or solving a specific problem – and you need to do this in a way that's effective, that's unique and that gets to the point quickly.

This is how you make your book 'meaty' rather than just a lot of waffle. What is it that your book is *really* doing? What is it that makes it different and unique? What value do you really bring to the table?

Using all this information you can structure your book and design it in such a way that people will want to keep reading...

How To Structure The Contents of Your eBook

A good place to start is with a rough outline of your book such as a table of contents. Note that this will likely change over time as you write.

That contents should start with an introduction and this is one of the most important aspects of your book – especially if you're giving away free previews. Your objective here is not to kill time treading water so that you can bulk out your word count. Instead, this should be where you hit home right away by selling the dream and outlining *precisely* what it is that your readers can expect to learn.

So if you have a fitness ebook, you start by telling *why* fitness is so important and by painting a picture of what life could be like if your readers were stronger, slimmer and fitter. If your book is more about solving a specific problem, then your aim is going to be to focus on that problem and to describe the pain point.

From there, you then outline the nature of your book and what makes it different. Ideally, you'll provide *some* kind of tip and some kind of value as you do this. That way, your audience will right away see that you're capable of delivering on your promises and will right away see that their money would be well-spent.

Finally, end by highlighting precisely what they can expect to learn if they keep reading and how that will help address the issues you've outlined.

Next you'll launch into the first chapter. In this part you need to provide the basic foundation that your readers will need to understand the rest of the book. So if you're writing about internet marketing, then you should explain *what* internet marketing is and how it works.

That means explaining the basic business model and a bit of the history. Conversely, if you're writing about this diet or that, then you should explain the essentials that your readers need to know regarding nutrition. That doesn't mean you need to write a science textbook, just make sure you're prepping the audience with the knowledge they need.

You might also outline the 'lay of the land' or the status quo in your particular niche.

Next you need to demonstrate *your* philosophy and what you're bringing to the table. Do you have a unique 'trick' that your audience can you? Do you have a better strategy than the one most people are subscribing to? This is where you differentiate yourself and put across the unique aspect to your book.

Now start outlining the precise steps and show your audience how to combine the basic knowledge with your unique approach and ideas. This might be one chapter or seven depending on the complexity of the topic.

And of course this doesn't necessarily have to be a 'unique strategy' as such – it might just as well be a unique way of displaying the information. If your book was a '10 step program' to launching a restaurant, then these chapters would be where you'd present that 10 step program.

Finally, you would deal with any additional thoughts, concerns or tips and offer any appendix, resources or other additional information.

You can vary your structure, but this is a fairly safe way to go. Let's recap on that:

1. **Introduction**
2. **Overview of the subject**
3. **Unique perspective/ideas/philosophy**
4. **Take-home action plan**
5. **Take-home action plan**

6. Take-home action plan

7. Additional tips and discussion

8. Resources and appendix

9. Conclusion

Outsourcing Your eBook

If you absolutely cannot write the book yourself though, then you might still opt to outsource the creation to someone else. This is a perfectly acceptable approach but remember what we said earlier: you will struggle to find someone who is an absolute expert in the niche you want to write about, which in turn is going to create challenges when it comes to offering something definitive or ground-breaking.

Make sure you look hard then for a writer who really knows their stuff and ask to see a sample of their writing before you order the full thing. Don't expect a writer to write for you for free of course! But consider ordering the first chapter or just one article before you pay for the whole book.

It's also a good idea to give them as much structure and instruction as possible. Allow them flexibility to move beyond the scope of your outline (the best structure for chapters etc. will evolve as they write) but at the same time make sure that they don't just have a subject matter but that they also understand the key points you want to get across, the style you want and any specific tips, ideas or advice you have.

Note as well that you'll obviously get what you pay for. It's worth paying a little more to get a writer who has 'the voice' and who really understands the subject matter, rather than paying less and getting something that has been outsourced overseas and is written in broken English.

If you do decide to outsource the writing process, then you can find writers on sites like UpWork.com. Just post your job and then once you've found someone, you can go through them directly in future.

Other Ways to Get Content

There are other ways to get your content too though! One option for example is to *reuse* content from your website. This is a smart trick that can actually be very profitable without rubbing anyone up the wrong way.

Think about it: if you have a blog that you've been running for the last 2 years, then chances are that you have something in the region of 100 articles on there. If those articles are 1,000 words long on average, then that's 100,000 words of content! And most of your visitors will not have read all of that content – especially the older stuff.

This means you can create a compendium of content using your old articles and also include some extra material and that way profit more from the work you've already done. If you're worried about complaints, you could even take *down* some of that old content.

This isn't quite as good as writing something from scratch and won't have that same value proposition or that same 'hook' by offering something truly new. But as a way to test the water for your book, it's an excellent option!

Some marketers will even make money by re-selling content that is in the public domain! As long as you are sure that the content doesn't have any restrictions, then there is no reason that you can't do this either.

The great thing about ebook content is that Google isn't going to index it. Google can't look at PDFs that you don't upload and that means you can't get into trouble for using the same content more than once.

Again, these aren't ideal strategies but if your intention is to make something you can use quickly... then it's certainly an option!

Buying Books

Finally, one more option is to buy a book you like. This might mean buying PLR content (private label rights) which you can edit and resell (there are lots of ebooks like this that are designed specifically to allow you to resell them as your own) or it might mean just contacting the author of an old book and asking if you can sell it online. This might mean splitting the profits but if it's a great book that hasn't found an audience, then you can be the one to turn it into a success and that can be very profitable!

Length and Other Factors

When writing your ebook, the longer you take, the more it is of course going to cost you. A good writer will often cost as much as $3-5 per 100 words. This means that a 10,000 word ebook might set you back $300 or $500. Likewise, if you write the book yourself, you will be investing more and more time, money and effort as you take longer to complete the book.

The length of your eBook needs to be as long as it needs to be.

You could write your story/ideas in just 10-20 pages if that's all it needs to be. You don't want to fluff it up just to increase the page numbers.

Nowadays, people have short attention spans because of the internet and amount of information that's out there.

Chapter 3

How to Write Compelling Content

If you *can* write the book yourself though, then note that this is always going to be the preferred approach. At the same time, bear in mind that you can always choose to go the 'middle way' and compromise. That is to say that you can write the book yourself and then have someone who is more of an expert on the matter proof read it for you.

The next question then is how you're going to make your own writing style engaging to read and something that people will want to sit through. Here are some pointers that can help you to write more engaging, interesting and entertaining content!

Writing Your Book

The next consideration is going to be your writing style. How do you go about creating a writing style that your readers will find gripping and that will convey all the information you need it to? What tone is right for your audience? How do you keep them reading?

There are lots of tips here. The first is simply to make sure that your book is *well written*. That means it should be free from spelling errors and other mistakes as far as possible. At the same time though, it also means that it should be written in a style that's suitable for the subject matter. If your book is very technical or professional, then you should write with a professional tone. If your book is a little more light-hearted then a conversational tone will be fine.

Either way though, the most important aim is readability. The big question is: is the book easy to read and follow? Does it engage the audience and is it entertaining? Every decision you make should serve these points.

Your book should flow quickly and be good to read – so you should never make decisions to try and 'sound professional' or to impress your audience. Avoid jargon and always try to say things as efficiently as possible with the fewest words necessary to get your exact meaning across.

A good way to test the readability for your book is to try reading it out loud to yourself. When you do this, you'll find that some sentences don't flow as well as they could or that the meaning doesn't come across easily. Rewrite those sentences to ensure that your book will sound right when it is spoken. If you can do this, then it should flow easily and should be entertaining for your readers.

At the same time:

- Consider using a narrative structure which will make your book more compelling and engaging

- Break large paragraphs up into lots of smaller sentences

- Speak directly to the reader (use lots of rhetorical questions, 'you' statements etc.)

- End paragraphs and sentences on cliff hangers to keep the reader moving to the next section

If you do all these things, then your book should be as engaging as possible.

How To Get Over The Dreaded Blank Page

Of course the other big challenge when it comes to writing an ebook is simply motivating yourself to keep writing and facing that dreaded 'blank page'. This is something that you will need to fight to overcome as a writer but note that some of the most prolific authors in history struggled with this problem.

So what do you do when you're staring down that blank page and you're not sure what to put there?

Well, when you find it difficult to write, one tip is to consider changing the format, the way you're introducing the topic or how you're starting the subject matter for that chapter. Often if you find it hard to write, it's because you find it boring and you can't bring yourself to sit down and struggle with that topic for however many words.

But think of it this way: if *you* find it boring to write, then what are the chances that your audience is going to find it interesting to read? In this scenario, you probably need to rethink the way you are writing the section to make it more interesting and more engaging. That will make it easier to write *and* more engaging to read!

Other than that, it comes down to discipline and to being able to force yourself to write for long periods of time without interruption. Try reading other books on the subject to put yourself in the mood and to let the writing style seep into your own your approach.

Chapter 4

Formatting – How to Create Stunning PDFs

If you're going to be selling your book on Kindle (something we'll look at later on), then you'll need to create your book in epub format. Otherwise, you'll be creating a PDF which can be read with Adobe reader.

Either way, the process is going to be largely similar and the objective is the same: to make your book look beautiful, to ensure it is easy to read and to get people to want to keep turning to the next page without getting bored.

Fortunately, creating great looking PDFs and ePub books is pretty easy...

How to Create a Formatted Document

The first thing you'll need to do is to invest in a copy of Word from Microsoft. While it *is* possible to make ebooks using other software, MR Word will make it considerably easier than any other tool and will provide you with all of the advanced formatting options and features that you will need to make a professional-looking end product.

To star with, make sure that you pick a font that looks crisp and easy to read. Just as with your writing style, the single most important objective here is to make sure that your content is readable and that means having a large typeface that is a pleasure to read. Arial is very popular, as is Calibri. Pick one of these and use a good font size.

From here, you'll want to separate your book into chapters, titles, headings, sub headings etc. Fortunately, Word offers an easy way to do this that has become the accepted industry standard.

Basically, you are going to highly any chapter titles and set them as 'Heading 1' using the option found in the home tab. Any subheadings within this chapter you are going to use 'Heading 2' for and any subheadings below *that* will be 'Heading 3'.

This will look the part and will ensure that your book looks appealing when you zoom out. At the same time though, you can also use these headings to quickly navigate around your book. Press 'Ctr + F' to open the navigation pane on the left hand of the screen and from there, you'll see that you can pick the headings and jump straight to them within your document.

This will help you when writing your article – and many different platforms such as Kindle will automatically recognize these as being chapter headings.

Better yet, using these types of headings means that you can very easily insert a table of contents that will be updated as you go. Simply head up to the top of your book and then select the 'References' tab. Now click 'Table of Contents' and select the style of contents you want. This is a great way to make your book look very professional with minimal work! Likewise, inserting a page header and page numbers is similarly easy. You can also use the 'Title' style for your book's main title and 'Subtitle' for the subtitle (no surprise there!).

Once you've done all this, you can also hit the Design tab in Word in order to find more options for changing the look of your book based on the titles etc. This can make a fairly big change to the way your book looks and feels and if you choose the colors next to it, you can come up with something unique.

Images

Another tip is to make sure that you insert lots of images. Breaking up your text with images, paragraphs and headers makes it much more readable but images can be used to make your book interesting and outstanding.

You can buy these images from stock image sites, you can find *free* stock image sites (such as freeimages.com) or you can create your own by taking photos.

Of course if you're willing to go one step further, then you can also outsource the creation of your images by using Fiverr.com, or one of the other freelancing sites that we've already discussed.

While it might feel like a waste of time creating a unique design, adding images and generally creating a look for your book; it can make a *huge* difference to your sales.

Try to think outside the box and really think of your ebook as a real *product*. Give it a distinct visual layout and a unique style. If you do this, you can strengthen your brand awareness and at the same time make something that people will be excited to read and proud to own.

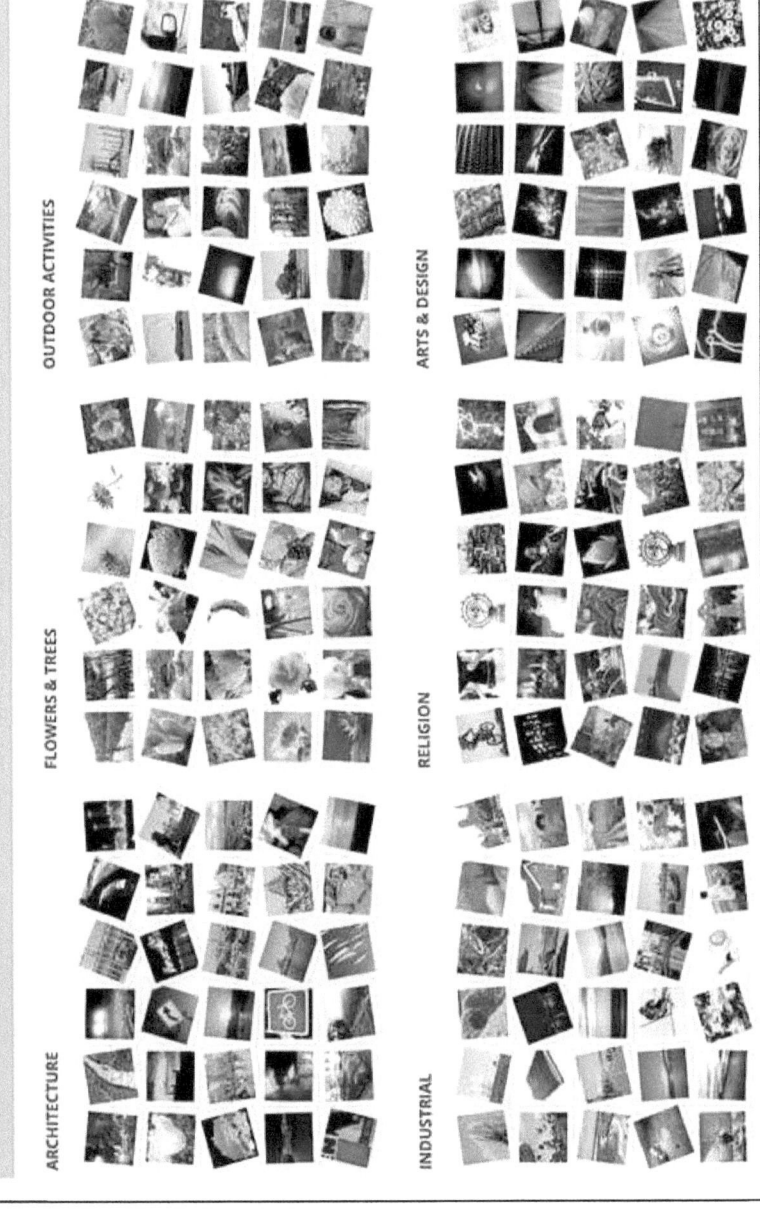

BROWSE 388,944 FREE PHOTOS AND ILLUSTRATIONS

OUTDOOR ACTIVITIES

ARTS & DESIGN

FLOWERS & TREES

RELIGION

ARCHITECTURE

INDUSTRIAL

41

This makes a huge difference to your sales – even in the way your own enthusiasm for the project will come across in your marketing materials. Once again – if you're proud of your book and excited about it, then that will come across in the text and your readers will be equally excited to read it and buy it!

Finally, save your book in PDF format or HTML if you're planning on selling it via Kindle.

Chapter 5

Designing Your Cover

Another important design feature that will have a big impact on your sales and your eventual success is the cover of your book. If you create a book with a great cover, then it will immediately stand out and people will be much more interested to read it.

The emphasis here should be on making your book look different and interesting. If all your book is is a block of text on a blank background, then it won't look highly professional or particularly interesting. Likewise though, if your book just has a generic image on the cover, then it will once again feel cheap and fail to have the impact you're aiming for.

Take a look at your local bookshop and try to identify the books that have the best job of standing out and looking interesting. You'll probably find that they are highly stylized, that they use very unique colorschemes or that they look futuristic or highly modern. Try and learn from these and use the same techniques in your own design.

Note as well though that your design will automatically have some unique differences due to the specific challenges of creating ebooks. For instance, it doesn't pay to have anything too complicated for your cover. If you do, then you will find that it looks cramped when the image is shrunken down, or that it looks bad when it is in black and white.

Your cover is very likely to be shown in black and white if you intend on selling it on Kindle, because most Kindle devices only have black and white e-ink displays. This means you need to ensure that your cover is going to be high contrast.

Even when this isn't the case, you'll probably often be showing your cover image as part of a small icon on your sales pages and that means you'll want it to shrink to a smaller size well while still being captivating and impressive.

How to Create a Great Cover

The next question then is *how* you're going to go about creating your cover. In terms of the best tools to use, it's worth investing in a copy of Adobe Photoshop if you can. Adobe offer a free trial at http://www.adobe.com/products/photoshop.html.

Next, you're going to need what's called an ebook 'action script'. This essentially creates realistic covers. One great product that offers a set of action script is called Cover Action Pro, available at http://www.coveractionpro.com

Installing is easy as it provides instructions. You simply design your cover.

Then the result will end up like the following image:

Outsourcing Your Cover Design

Once again though, there's a good chance that all this will be beyond you. If you are someone who doesn't consider themselves to be a designer, then consider outsourcing the process via a freelancing platform.

Some popular sites to go to are www.fiverr.com and www.upwork.com. On Fiverr, you'll find many freelancers available to design a cover for $5.

Graphics & Design | Digital Marketing | Writing & Translation | Video & Animation | Music & Audio | Programming & Tech | Advertising | Business | Lifestyle | Gifts | Fun & Bizarre | Other

Shop Category

All in Graphics & Design
Book Covers & Packaging
Show More

Delivery Time
Up to 24 hours
Up to 3 days
Up to 7 days
○ Any

Online Status
Show Online Sellers

Cover Type
Book Cover
Product Packaging
Product Label
Show More

Packshot
2D graphic
3D model
Animated model

File Format
JPG
PNG
PDF
Show More

Package Includes
Source File
Commercial Use
Print Ready
Show More

High Rating   Recommended   New

I will design an Eye Catching Ebook or Kindle Cover with   A$13.21

I will make you Cool Kindle or eBook Cover   A$6.60

I will make an eBook Kindle, Book Cover or 3D in 24 hours   A$6.60

I will make eBook Cover with Gifts   A$6.60

I will design professional ebook covers 3D software   A$6.60

I will design AMAZING product label   A$19.81

I will do a book cover or a movie poster flyers for you   A$6.60

I will design a CREATESPACE, a Kindle Cover   A$6.60

I will create a 3D ebook cover   A$6.60

I will design you an awesome book cover   A$19.81

I will design 2 Ebook Cover in 24 Hours   A$6.60

I will design PROFESSIONAL Ebook Cover or Kindle Cover   A$6.60

Chapter 6

Selling Your Ebook Through A Website

Okay! So now you have your well-written ebook in a great niche, with a very compelling title and eye-grabbing cover. You're well on your way to becoming very successful!

The next challenge though is to find an audience for that book and help it to sell!

And the most common way that a lot of marketers will do this is through content marketing – which essentially means creating a website, creating lots of content and building a big audience that will trust you as a thought leader in your niche.

The general idea here is to gradually build trust and authority to the point where your audience will consider paying to get more of your content. You are offering *free* content in the form of blog posts, videos and more and this is then going to give them the confidence in your ability to provide information and advice.

To see how this works, it can be helpful to imagine the process that a new user might take when they go from discovering your website, to then buying your book.

So let's say you have an ebook on home bodyweight workouts. You then create a website and fill it with lots of new blog posts about working out and building muscle.

Then, one web user discovers your website while searching for information. Perhaps they're looking for unique ways to train their pecs, or maybe they're looking for diet advice for home workouts. Either way, they search on Google for that keyword and they find an article on your website. They then read that article and find your post, which they find entertaining and informative. At that point, they notice the name of your blog before leaving.

Then they might come across your content *again* when doing a related search on Google another time. And perhaps they might find an article written by you on social media being recommended by a friend. Each time they see your content, they are impressed and make a note to read more of your writing in future.

Eventually, they become so familiar with your brand and they trust you so much as a resource that they start searching your site *specifically* for answers to their questions. They then might go on to subscribe to your newsletter, or to potentially bookmark your site.

Either way, they are now officially a fan of your blog and of you as a writer. This means that they are more likely to see when you start promoting your new ebook and they are more likely to be interested and to go ahead and make the purchase!

It's a lengthy process as you can see, but by consistently generating high quality content, you can build a bigger and bigger following and potentially sell them lots of products over the course of that time.

How to Set Up Sales Through Your Website

All this of course also means that you're going to need a means of selling your books and products through your website. One of the best ways to do this is by creating an online store of some sort and in that regard, you have two main options.

One option is to create a basic ecommerce store, which will work like Amazon or any other website selling items online –

the only difference is that you're going to be selling digital product rather than physical ones.

Doing this is relatively easy too – if you have a WordPress website then you can sell digital products by installing WooCommerce which is a plugin that will turn your blog *into* an ecommerce store.

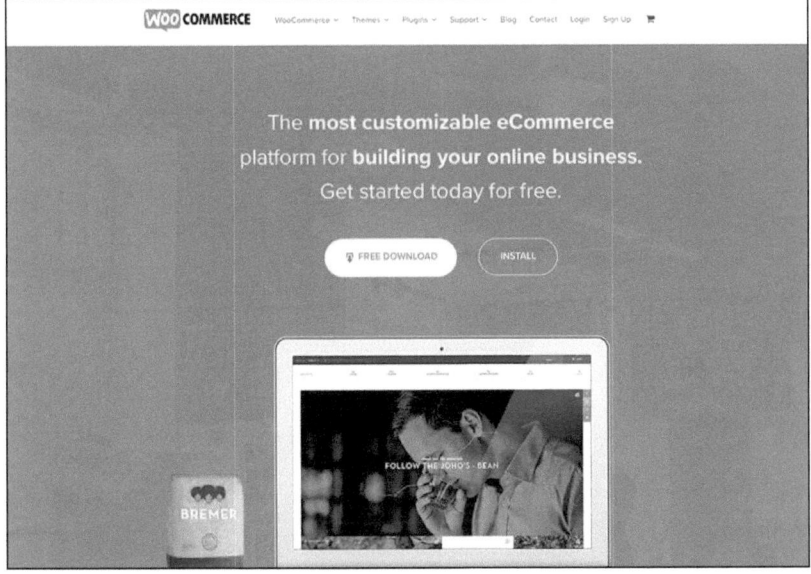

Another option is to set up a 'sales page'. This is a single page that will be completely dedicated to selling the one product. That means the page will contain no other information, no adverts and no distractions: the entire thing is designed *purely* to sell your book. We'll look more at how to create this kind of landing page later on. Likewise, we'll discuss techniques you can use to promote your website and to encourage more sales as a result.

Chapter 7

Selling Your Ebook Through Kindle

Another option for selling your ebook is to sell it on Kindle. This is a great option as it means that anyone who owns a Kindle can now search for your title and then download it. This also means that they can buy from a vendor that they already trust and where their details are likely already stored (Amazon). It streamlines the whole process and opens you up to a massive audience that will include a much broader set of demographics. This is ideal if you have an ebook on a specific career for instance.

54

Considerations

Before you go ahead and add your ebook to Kindle, note that there are a few considerations to bear in mind. The first of these is that you can risk cannibalizing your own sales. What this means is that if you are selling your ebook from your website for $35 and you're also selling it on Kindle for $10, you might find that people buy the Kindle version instead of the one on your website. Often this will be the case, seeing as Kindle books tend to sell for much less than PDFs from websites.

Even if you sell the two books at the same price though, it's important to bear in mind that Kindle takes quite a big cut (you choose between 35- 70%). This means that you'll still make more money selling the book on your own.

So that means you will likely want to price the Kindle version *above* your own version, in which case you'll make fewer sales. Again though, this all comes down to your niche and your target demographic. If your book is about knitting, price it low on Kindle and even lower on your website – aiming to sell primarily through Kindle where there are more older readers.

But if your book is on making money online, then you should price it *high* on your website and even higher on Kindle.

You might not make many sales on Kindle this way, but it certainly doesn't *hurt* to have the book on the site as you might generate the odd sale or two.

One other option? Make two different versions of your ebook! This is actually particularly smart if you plan on joining Kindle Select, as this program requires you to make your book exclusive to Kindle.

Prepping Your Book for Kindle

Now you know what the risks and pitfalls of selling a book on Kindle is, how do you go about going ahead if you still intend to?

The first step is to get your ebook ready for 'Kindle Format 8'. This basically ensures that your book will be easily read and understood by Amazon in order to be converted into a Kindle file. If you use the formatting guide from earlier in this book, then you'll be ready right away to upload to Kindle Direct Publishing, which is completely free and *should* be a very easy and straightforward process. All you need to do is to save the file first as 'Web Page, Filtered' or 'Web Page'.

You can read the full formatting guidelines here: https://kdp.amazon.com/help?topicId=A17W8UM0MMSQX6

There are also a number of other things you can do to ensure your book will meet the formatting guidelines though. For instance, you should make sure that all your chapters start on new pages by using page breaks. You might also choose to add some of the types of pages/sections that Amazon recommends:

• A title page – A centered title with your sub-title and your name (or the author's name if you are not they)

• A copyright page – Include any copyright or legal notices here. Note that you automatically own copyright to anything that you create yourself. If you are commissioning the work, then you need to ensure that it is specifically stated that you will own the full copyright to the text once it is completed.

• Dedication – This is up to you but can be a nice touch that adds professionalism.

• Preface – This usually goes just after your dedication.

• Prologue – A little introduction that is normally inserted just after the preface.

• Bibliographies

• Appendices

• Notes

- Glossaries

Note that images need to be inserted by going to insert > image rather than being copied and pasted. They should be inserted in the center of the page too – don't try to use word wrap or anything else fancy like that.

Submitting Your Book to Amazon

To submit your book to Kindle Direct Publishing, just go to kdp.amazon.com. This process is completely free and very easy. Just click 'Create New Title' to get started.

From here, you'll then be presented with some more fields where you can enter additional information. The required information includes:

- the book name
- subtitle
- series title
- volume number
- edition number
- language
- author
- publisher

- contributors
- ISBN (if you've purchased one)
- categories
- publishing rights (don't check that your book is in the public domain or you will waiver your copyright!)

You'll also be able to add some information such as a description and a cover on your listing. This is very important for encouraging maximum sales and the main objective should be to convey the 'value proposition' that you're offering. Again: how does your book make people's lives better?

What can it offer that other books can't?

You'll also be asked to input your price. Remember what we discussed earlier regarding competing with yourself and consider the commission that Amazon will be taking. Note that Amazon normally takes 35% for cheaper books but this goes up to 70% for more expensive titles. You can also elect to give away 70% commission for your sales in which case there are a *few* perks – for instance this means that you'll still gain the full price for your book even when Amazon chooses to put it on offer.

Maximizing Sales and Ranking

When it comes to maximizing sales on Kindle, the main objective is to increase your ranking on the Kindle store, which is an extension of Amazon itself.

This means you may want to reconsider the way you title your book. Essentially, the Kindle store and Amazon both work just like Google. This is fundamentally a search engine and people come here to find content by searching for what they're looking for.

That means that you can actually increase your visibility and thus your sales by thinking about your title in terms of search terms and what people will be looking for. If your book is called 'Fitness Masterclass' then it might not get too many people discovering it by searching for the phrase. But if your book is called 'Home Bodyweight Workouts' then it might.

Of course the problem with *that* option is that it will be going up against a lot of competition. Again, the key is to pick something that is in demand and that gets a lot of searches but that doesn't face too much competition from other sales.

Other than this, what will most strongly affect your visibility in the store is:

- The number of downloads

- The reviews

Your objective then is to get as many downloads as possible and to gain as many positive reviews as you can as well.

One way to increase your positive reviews is simply to ask people to leave a review if they enjoyed your content. Don't bribe them or try and trick them into doing this as this can get you penalized. Simply point out in your content that it would help you a great deal if they genuinely enjoyed your book – otherwise your readers might not think to do it! Otherwise, you can also ask your fans to do the same from your own website.

Another pointer is to sell your book cheaply to begin with. You can alter the price at any time and what this means is that you can actually sell your book at a low price for a while to generate the maximum sales and then increase the cost once you're ranking right at the top. Note as well that running promotions and selling your book cheaply for a while is a great way to get good reviews – if you are selling your book for $1 and it's offering a ton of great content, then people will likely be so impressed that they'll be moved to leave positive feedback.

If you *do* opt to sign up for Kindle Select then this can also help a great deal to make it easier for you to promote your book. Books on Kindle Select will often get special promotions and will be featured by Amazon which can help you to drive a lot of sales and give you the initial spark you need to get going.

Either way, note that on Kindle, it really does help to take an initial hit in terms of pricing in order to get the momentum you need to sell more further down the line.

Chapter 8

More Ways to Sell Your Ebook

There are actually many more ways you can sell an ebook and this is something that a lot of people overlook.

Once you've invested that amount of time, effort and/or money into creating your book, it makes sense to maximize your returns by selling it in as many places as possible. And each time you find a new platform to sell your book from, you will reach a new audience and create new opportunities to hit the big time!

Selling in Hard Copy

One particularly interesting option is to create a hardcopy version of your book! This is something that's actually very possible now thanks to 'POD' or 'Print On Demand' publishing. Back in the day, publishing a book meant ordering thousands of copies and then trying to sell them at a profit – of course this is a strategy that is very risky and often doomed to failure.

But with POD, books are only printed each time you make a sale. That means that there is no up-front cost. Sure, the printer will take a commission and you'll be charged for the shipping and materials, but you only make profit each time your book sells. That means you can then offer something physical and tangible to your readers and this can make a *huge* difference in terms of sales – especially if you are targeting an audience that is less tech savvy and less on-board with buying digital-only products.

This then creates many more avenues for selling your book too – you can even try and sell it in person from a highstreet store, or sell it from a carboot sale! Just being able to show people the product for real can also help you generate even more sales even when those sales end up being digital (in other words, it can be used purely as a marketing tool).

To create a hardcopy version of your book, just head to Amazon's self- publishing section, or try Lulu.com. There are plenty of options for creating the type of book you want (hardback, floppy back, A5, A4, color, black and white etc.) and the whole process is surprisingly easy.

Other Platforms

There are also many other platforms through which you can sell your ebook and each one provides you with a way to expand your audience and to create new ways for people to discover you.

The Kindle Store is what you call a 'distribution platform' and if you create a hardcopy of your book with Lulu, then you'll also be in the Lulu store for people to discover. At the same time though, you can also promote your book via Google Play Books, via iTunes or via Nook (a competitor to Amazon). Unless you have signed some kind of agreement, there is absolutely no reason not to be present on *all* of these platforms and to thereby really maximize your sales potential.

You can also opt to somewhat go-it-alone and to sell in non-conventional ways. For instance, why not just create a listing on eBay? There's no rule against it and in fact you'll find that a great many authors sell their books this way! Another option is to sell directly to your audience through your mailing list or through social media!

Heck, if you're really ambitious and you have an idea for a book that you think is truly unique and exciting then you could even try and raise the money for it on Kickstarter which would also be a great way to get people excited for it and to get some media exposure!

Chapter 9

How to Build a Killer Sales Page To Sell Your Ebook

If you're going to sell your ebook from your own website, then the best way to do that is often with a sales page. As stated earlier, this is essentially a single page on your website that is entirely dedicated to shifting copies of your book and encouraging people to download. That means that the entire design of the page will revolve around the 'Buy Now' button (called an action button) and it means that the copy itself will be expertly crafted to motivate people to want to do likewise.

The objective of your sales page is maximize 'conversions'. This means that for every person who visits the page, you want to maximize the likelihood that they're going to make a purchase. This in turn gives you one single place where you can focus your marketing and your advertising.

So for example, if your sales page has a conversion rate of 10%, that means that you can send 100 people to the page using ads and expect to make 10 sales. This is a very high conversion rate, but it is possible!

The reason this is so effective is that it means you can then come up with a solid business plan based on somewhat concrete numbers. If you were to create a marketing campaign using Facebook Ads or Google AdWords for instance, then you would be charged 'per click'. That means that you would only pay each time someone clicked on your ad and that means that you know exactly how much 100 visitors would cost you. Say your 'CPC' (cost per click) is 0.50 cents and you get 10 sales for every 100 clicks, that means you can calculate that you're getting each sale for $5. If your book sales for $10, then that means you're making 50% profit!

Of course the numbers won't always be so favourable and finding a strategy on Google AdWords or Facebook Ads that works can involve spending a fair bit of your budget to get things just right.

However, this is the objective and this is the basic reason that having a sales page works so well!

So how do you go about creating such a page?

Designing Your Sales Page

In terms of designing your sales page, the most popular approach is to make the design long and narrow. The idea behind this is that a long narrow page encourages the visitor to keep scrolling down the page and to keep looking further. This feeling of scrolling in turn makes them feel more and more committed to your product. By the time they get to the end, it will feel like a waste to go back to the start again without buying anything!

As mentioned, everything about this site should be pointing at your action button in order to maximize your conversions. That means there should be no other advertisement on the page and no links back to your homepage or any other part of your site. The only way to leave this page should be to click the 'Buy' button or to click back.

Another common aspect of these pages is that they utilize a red or orange color scheme a lot of the time. The idea behind this is that these colors raise the heartrate and make us more impulsive and more prone to action. This is a good thing when you're trying to make sales as actually most things we buy we buy impulsively and based on emotion rather than logic. Your objective is to get a rapid sale and a big red button does this better than a big blue one!

If you want to create a sales page quickly and easily, you can do so by using the theme for WordPress called 'Optimize Press'.

You can then use 'Otpimizely' in order to 'split test' the design. This means that you're creating two almost identical designs for your sales page and then tweaking one of them slightly.

Now half of your visitors will be sent to each version of the site and you can observe which site performs better in terms of conversion rate. If the change helped you get more conversions, then you adopt it across all versions of the sales page and you try introducing a new change. This way you can 'evolve' your design to be perfectly designed to maximize sales and this can see your conversion rates climb from 0.01% to 1% to 10%!

Persuasive Writing for Your Sales Page

The next piece of the puzzle is to use persuasive copy in order to encourage your visitors to buy your books.

The first thing to make sure you do here is to capture the attention of your visitors and then to hold it. Your aim is to reduce your 'bounce rate' (number of people who leave your site after 2 seconds) and you do this by grabbing them right away with a compelling pitch.

One way to do this is with a 'narrative structure'. That means that you're going to talk about your product as though it were a story. Discuss how you 'were once overweight' or tell your visitors your rags to riches tale. Not only is this very inspiring and very effective at getting an emotional response, but we are naturally designed to listen to stories and that means that the strategy is often very effective at preventing people from leaving your page!

From here, the focus is then going to be on that value proposition. We've addressed this concept several times before but this is where it is most important of all.

Your aim is to make your book sound life changing and to get your readers to imagine and visualize what their lives could be like if they make the purchase. Talk about how it would feel to have incredible abs and endless energy, or get them to picture what it would be like to have their own restaurant and to feel proud of their accomplishments.

At the same time though, you also need to show them how your book can make this happen. Explain what's in the book and make sure to address any concerns that your audience might have. In other words, how do they know your book isn't just another set of empty promises? What makes this different from every other book on the market?

You can do this by addressing concerns head on before your readers think of them and also by using social proof, authority quotes and facts and figures. Another very good strategy is to minimize the risk involved in buying your product by offering a money-back guarantee or a free sample.

If you do this, you'll find that it helps to remove the concerns but that very few people actually take you up on the offer to refund their purchase.

Last but not least, make sure that you encourage a rapid decision by creating urgency and scarcity. You do this by saying you have limited stock or by introducing a limited-time discount. Either way, your aim is to make your visitors buy right away rather than going away to think about it!

Chapter 10

How To Promote Your eBook
And Increase Sales

Now you have your book for sale on multiple platforms and you know how to really push that value proposition to make people want it. Hopefully you already know how to build a sales page and you should have an idea as to how you can rank more highly on Kindle.

But there are a few more strategies you can use to drive more sales, no matter which of these strategies you are using. Here are some of the best options…

Set Up an Affiliate Program

If you set up an affiliate program, this basically means that people can sell your book on your behalf and keep a percentage of the profit. This basically means you can build an army of marketers to help you make more sales and when you do that, you'll be able to double, triple or quadruple your turnover!

JVZoo, Clicbank and Commission Junction are all sites that allow you to do this. Head over to those sites and look at setting up an account as a product creator.

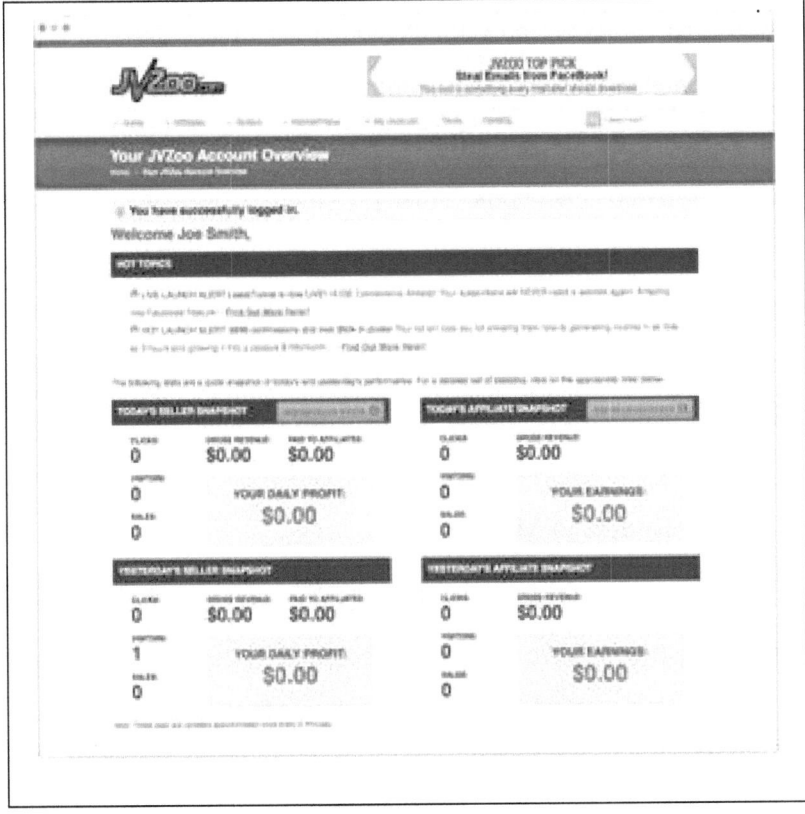

Use Google AdWords and Facebook Ads

We've already touched briefly on using CPC advertising in order to drive more sales to your products. This basically means that you're paying for clicks on your ads and don't pay anything otherwise. Making things even easier is the option to set a budget and to decide how much you're willing to pay for each click (though if you don't pay enough, your ad won't be seen!).

Perhaps the best option out of the two here is to use Facebook Ads. Facebook Ads provides a lot of advanced targeting options that lets you decide *precisely* who sees your ads. You can decide which gender, which location, what interests, what job title and more and ensure this way that only people who are already likely to buy your product see it!

Find Routes to Market

If you have a specific niche for your book (which you definitely should have – as we discussed at length!) then you should be able to find 'routes to market'. This means finding a direct channel to the people who are most likely to buy your product. If you are selling a knitting book, then that might mean a magazine or forum about knitting. If it's CrossFit you're writing about, then it might mean going to the CrossFit page on Facebook or the Google+ group.

Either way, creating an ebook for a specific group and then finding a way to reach them directly is a perfect business model and can drastically increase your sales.

Create a Freebie

Consider creating a shorter, free ebook that you can give away from your blog or website. Do this via a mailing list sign up form or anything else and basically use it as a way to demonstrate your quality and as a way to encourage more people to subscribe.

Another option sit to create a very cheap *paid* ebook, which can have the handy benefit of removing any reservations your audience might have about using your payment system. They're more likely to risk a $2 purchase and once they've done that, their details will be stored and they'll be comfortable with buying from you – making it far easier for you to sell bigger items in future.

CONCLUSION & ACTION PLAN

So there you go – that's everything you need to know in order to start selling your books and making a big profit from them. We've been through every single step, from conceiving the initial idea for your book and choosing a niche and a title, to actually writing your book and then trying to sell it in as many ways as possible.

There's a lot to take on board there, so I recommend reading through it all one step at a time as you create your product and take it to market.

But if there's one key take-home point, then it should be to make sure that your book offers some real *value*. This begins right from the moment when you choose the title and when you choose the niche. Pick a popular niche you can sell in, but more than that, make sure that you are providing something new and something worthwhile. Ensure that your book is unique and that it has something different to offer. Make sure that you solve a clear problem or offer some kind of real 'value proposition' so that your book demonstrably makes life better for the people reading it.

Make your book into a real *product* as well. This shouldn't be just a piece of writing saved as a PDF. This should be a beautiful example of formatting and writing with a stunning cover image and lots of great pictures and tables. Make something you're proud of!

If you can do this and you can then promote that to the right audience, then your sales will come and they will grow over time.

And then you can repeat the process all over again! Welcome to the world of digital publishing.

Printed by Libri Plureos GmbH in Hamburg,
Germany